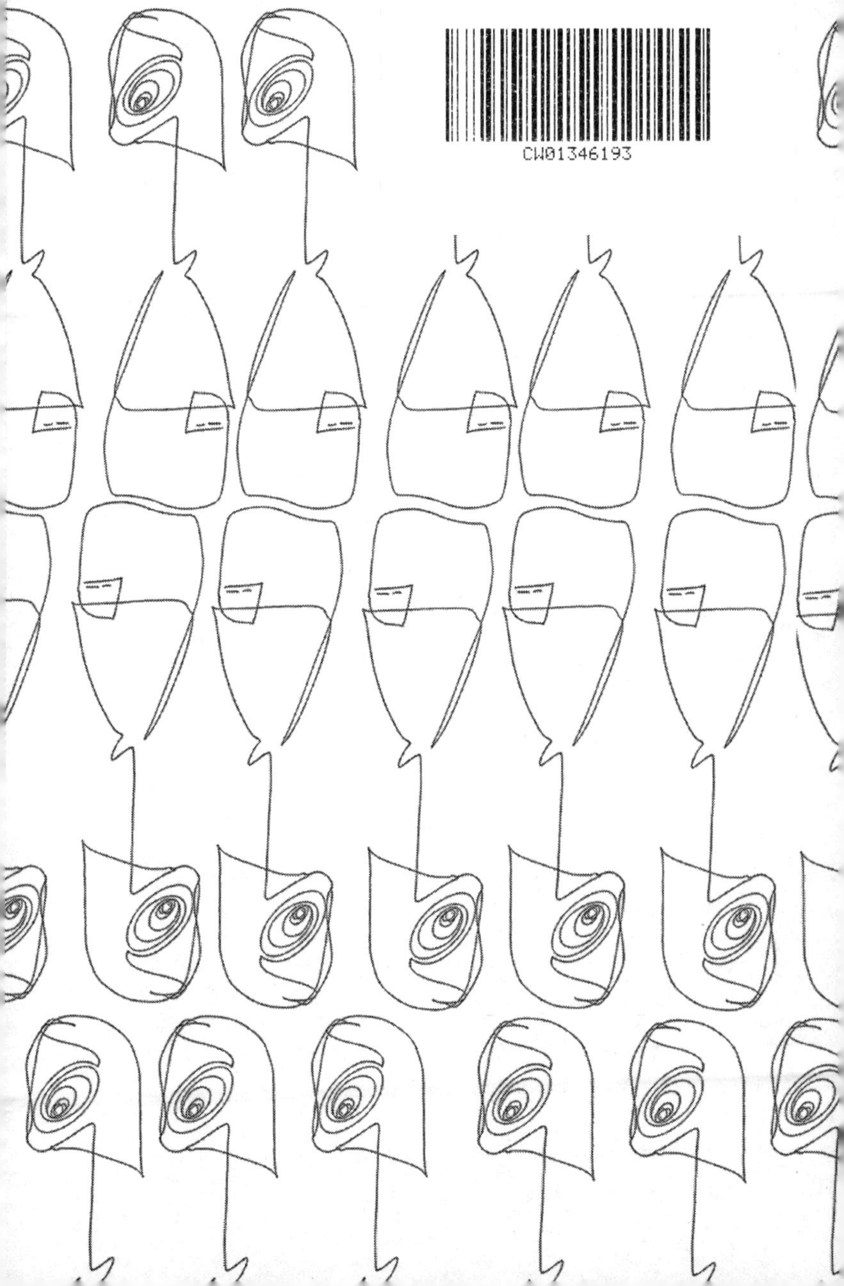

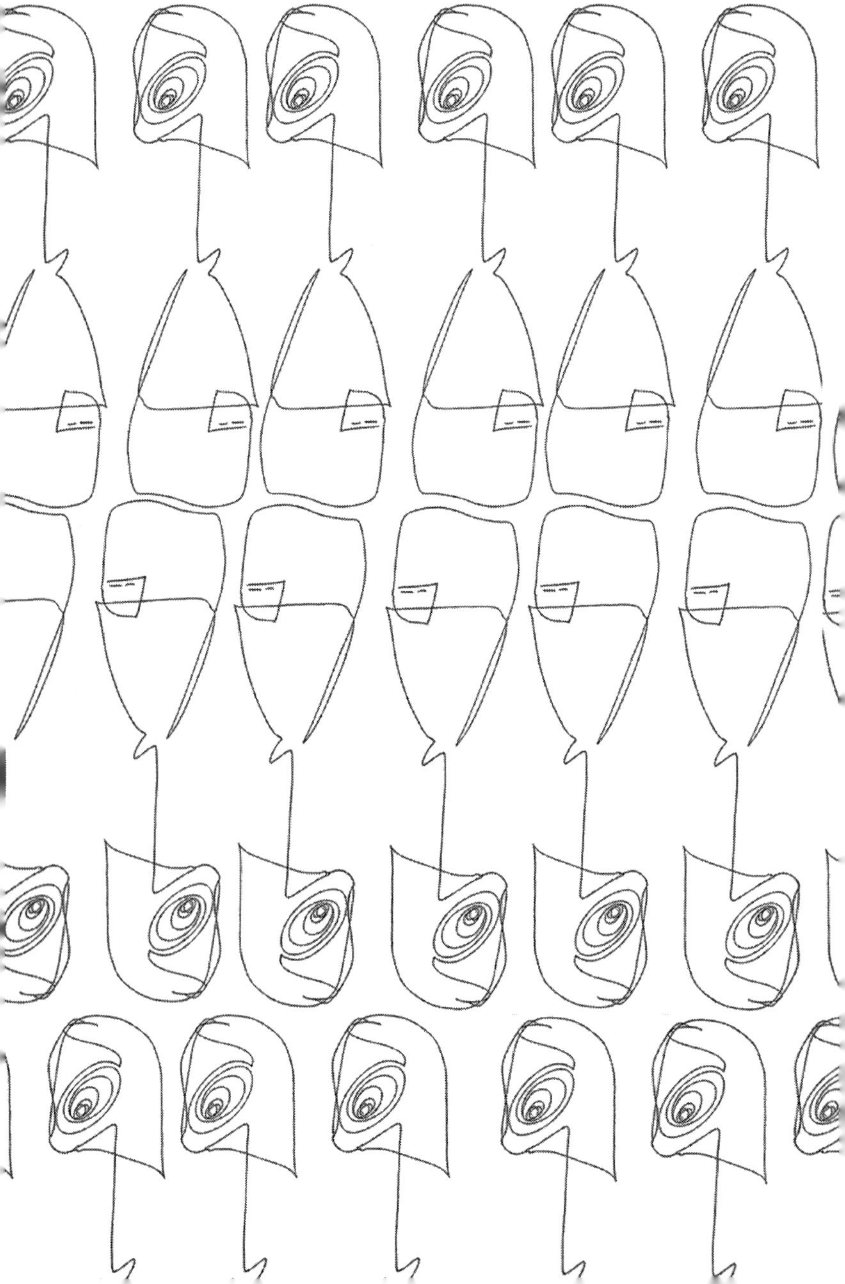

To Tom

The Chelsea Flower Show Massacre

Let 1000 flowers bloom!

Mark Fiddes

Mark Fiddes

Templar Poetry

First Published 2015 by Templar Poetry
Fenelon House
Kingsbridge Terrace
58 Dale Road, Matlock, Derbyshire
DE4 3NB
www.templarpoetry.co.uk

ISBN9781906285470

Copyright © Mark Fiddes 2015

Mark Fiddes has asserted his moral right to be identified as the author
of this work in accordance
with the Copyright, Designs and Patents Act 1988

All rights reserved. This book is sold subject to the condition
that it shall not, by way of trade or otherwise, be lent, resold, hired out
or otherwise circulated without the publisher's prior consent, in any form
of binding or cover other than that in which it is published and without
a similar condition including this condition being imposed on
the subsequent purchaser.

For permission to reprint or broadcast these poems write to Templar Poetry

A CIP catalogue record of this book is available from the British Library.

Typeset by Pliny
Printed and bound in England

For Margaret, Chris and Clare

Acknowledgments are due to the editors of the following publications in which some of these poems first appeared: *Live Canon Anthology* (The Chelsea Flower Show Massacre) 2014, *Frogmore Papers 84* (In the Valley of the Fallen) 2014.

Contents

The Chelsea Flower Show Massacre	1
Solo Doloroso	3
Sons of the Golden Section	5
A Pathology of Work	7
The Eternal Recurrence of Northbound Trains	8
The Existence of Dog	10
How to make Pan Catalan	12
In the Valley of the Fallen	13
Keep Britain Untidy	15
From Siberia	16
The Night Watch Man	18
Have we won yet?	20
The Page of Revelations	21
This is not a scam	22

The Chelsea Flower Show Massacre

The butterflies get in for free,
like the Queen, ex officio.
For bankers it's a hundred quid
per slick Savile Row carapace.
Same again for their *plus guests*
cocooned in crushed silk Gucci
thrilling to every sip of Moet
and the quadrille of canapés.

We follow a late Red Admiral
through the Fiorelli trelliswork
over the Swarovski fountain
jetting Perrier and rose petals
to the Fragonard tribute swing
that put the W in horticulture
styled by the crimping, pimping
manicurists of Bulgari.

Circling the Prada ha-ha
we alight in a cash-scented glade
cooing with fresh bonuses.
Here they will raffle gilded tickets
to paradise, Wagner and the moon.
A locker room of matey autographs
will be auctioned, faked by agents

in limos speeding between deals.
And it's all for Race Horse Rehab.
Watch the Oligarchs take the lead
past the Hedge Fund boys by a Rolex
snapping up Lord Coe's lucky shorts
and a small village near Cambridge
before the pheasant shoot with U2
goes to the Emperor of Tat
on whose sweatshops the sun never sets.

The air, swollen with generosity
now bursts in thundering ululation.
A Saxon thane shaking with battle-axe
stumbles from the shrubbery.
"Fukka!" he snarls, like he's lost his keys
before hacking through the buddleia
to the juice bar where gap year waiters
smoke their final cigarettes.

Solo Doloroso

(On George Clooney announcing his wedding plans)

"He's been taken," she says,
"by a human rights lawyer.
"It's just not fair."

She attempts to stack
the mechanically unstackable
metallic capsules of coffee
which tumble like command modules
from a failed lunar landing.

"I told you he wasn't gay,"
she says, as if it was my fault,
his heterosexuality.

*Espresso, Ristretto, Lothario,
Cunnilingo, Fellatio, Shtuppio*
from strong to soft, daily he came
in multiple flavours and accents
without mess or recrimination.

"It won't last," she says.
"What will they talk about all day?
"Torture?"

Under the rack of dried spices
the Nespresso has been eviscerated.
That plug I once fixed, ripped away.
A granular slag heap in the drip tray
now spills a Lake Como of tears.

I offer tea.
She snorts.
George Clooney has left the kitchen.

Sons of the Golden Section

I see my Dad through his forest
of paintbrushes, always marching
against the latest Dunsinane -
Aldermaston, Third Airports,
Wind Farmers, Greedy Bastards.
He was born against their grain
hewn into an Arcimboldo portrait
of fierce coppice with Beltane eyes
like the sign at The Green Man pub,
now a Travelodge on the A43.
He works paint with palette knives
as if colour, like a growing thing,
needed pruning and deadheading.
Druid roots creep through
his compositions, spiked with ivy
curdled with moonlight
including me his winter son
born on the stroke of a frozen Solstice.

This Father's Day, he gathers us
in his studio, a kingdom of turpentine,
skulls and masks, where he explains
to his grandson The Golden Section
from the snail's helix to seed heads,
faces, petals, pine cones, hurricanes,

galaxies, DNA, Pi and Fibonacci.
He draws the magic in charcoal
on flaking plaster, inciting those spirits
he hires from Pan, Orpheus and the gang
for his own savage geometries.
Like all the other men born of war
he has learned to apportion love
as if we lived in a time of rationing.
I now see his Golden Section applied
to the rest of us, each with our spiral
our rectangle and harmonious purpose
distanced along a grazed horizon
each with our own vanishing point.

A Pathology of Work

There's work that breaks your back
and work that cracks your soul
makes you perspire inside
behind the eyes, sliding down
your bones to corrode the heart
and short-circuit the nerves
allowing the senses to atrophy
even Smell with its prickled skein
through your own labyrinths.
Over many pay cheques this trickle
deposits human salt into the hollows
where glistening stalactites grow
of envy, fear, greed and self-esteem
often mistaken for character.
You will have sniffed this inner sweat
in the soggy folds of banknotes
the only place where millionaires share
their human stain with the poor.
After another brittle reconciliation
you ask where my tears hide.
I explain there's nothing left to cry.
These eyes are as dry as orchard leaves
after the last wasps and windfalls.
This soul has been worked to its knees.
There's nothing left to be freed
but the spine's still worth a burden,
if the price is right.

The Eternal Recurrence
of Northbound Trains

Dodging the drift of the witless
you dart down Platform 2
as a trout over stones smoothed
by decades to a favoured spot
lodged inches from the blunt edge
which bears your imprint the way
Hollywood stars leave their hands
in concrete on a pavement
praying for eternity.
Your cast fits under the flint chip
filling with rush, blur and black grit
crumbled from tunnel crust
and the urban burr of millions daily
colliding in soft particle contact.

Sometimes this bit of you winks
in the headlights of trains
or flashes for the photo finish
of a handicap too close to call
or shrinks to a claw in a crack.
Yet your gist survives
by the Passenger Safety Line
Blanco thick as a guard's belt.
So even when the platform north slips

into the Abyss of deep space
slammed by gangster planets
shattered by malevolent asteroids
then shat out by black holes
the Cosmos will still extol you
doing your best to Mind the Gap.

The Existence of Dog

More photocopy than dog
black and sharp, he scissored the street,
a Braque cut-out on whipcord,
leashed to his sluggish mistress,
an embleachment of hair and jeans.
Each night we renewed our distance.
Me, tethered to my own mindings
but always offering a whistle
in return for his whispery skip.
She, muttering whatever runes
she was reading from the pavement
until they stopped by my doorstep
one whizz bang night around Guy Fawkes'.

He was squatting like a rocket
spooling out more excrement
than his slenderness would allow
as if his anus were a rip
in the curtain of the Universe
through which a nearby Galaxy,
made only of shit, was fly tipping.
The poo turret grew slick and white
like classic shite from dogs of yore
who lived off scraps and groundsman's chalk
before they ate better than us.

In his eyes, the terror of birth
as he watched the future squeeze out
irreversible and needy.
She, gloving her hand in a Tesco's bag
flexed her surgical fingers
and clamped the dump with a snap.
"Every little helps," said I to the dog
now as hollow as parentheses
keening for kind words and a warm lap.
"Stay away from Benny!" she yelled.
With a yank on his strap they turned
leaving behind a canine fissure
the pucker in my 'ology of dog
that smiles every time I fuss over
what the hell I'm doing here.

How to make Pan Catalan

Unclasp your garlic gingerly
Place the pink-ribbed corset aside
If the nudity of the bulb offends
Opt for the soup or pâté alternative
Grip the clove's belly like a pen
Rasp back and forth over the toast
Releasing its hot breath. Rub on
Until flesh shreds and fingers stick
Now select the paunchiest tomato
Slack as velvet and long on the vine
Squeeze the seed sack until it bursts
Mash over the crusted furrows
Gloss with green oil
Spray with a necklace of sea salt
Exchange for stars
From the night-eyed woman
Sitting opposite, bare footed
Repeat a thousand times
Through harvest years and fallow
Until the last unclasping

In the Valley of the Fallen

(Dedicated to Josep Sunyol 1898 – 1936)

Dust waifs across the slabs
where Falangists still gather
to remember the Caudillo
once a year with hats and flags
under a thicket of tilted arms.
A susurrus stirs the pines
"Generalissimo" it whispers
like a nurse to a pillow.
"Generalissimo" it expires
like the prisoners of his war
forced to build this mausoleum
into the belly of the mountain
refilling the quarried stone
with their own skin and bone
veined and quiet as marble.

At the entrance to the tomb
a boy kicks a ball at the column
wearing the *blaugrana* shirt
of the team whose lefty President
was murdered down the road
eighty years away as the crow flies.
"Pass," I say. He lobs. I nod back.
His shot arcs bright as a sabre

across the shadow-spilling steps.
"Goooooooooaaaaaaalllllaaazo!"
He condors away on Stuka wings
and thermals of fanatic glory.
I shiver, halted and haunted
not by ghosts but the drip
of this calcite moment.

Keep Britain Untidy

(A Public Information message to the Little England Party)

This island has always leaked.
That's why its seas are the colour of dead warriors.
Although the fields appear swept
they're as rucked and seamed as a poor night's sleep
sprayed with reckless foliage
more Abstract Expressionist than picturesque.
Every city's made from jigsaw bits,
lost corners, famous holes and knackered two ply.
All attempts at planned growth
end up the butt of clever jokes or get bombed to shit.
Grey depots sprout like fungi
crammed with mini depots destined for other depots
along the cardiac auto routes
a triumph of cholesterol over mass circulation.
Even the Royals beget a wobbly line -
beheaders, dandies, philanderers and prudes
united only by horse adoration
under a patchwork flag of borrowed saints' ensigns.

The front door never closes - the Romans lost the key
so we never put the rubbish out:
it's mulched back into the steaming heap we call England
then trodden back in by some Ancient Feet.

From Siberia

                    these geese trail
              winter like needles pulling
        thread through sailcloth, salted
              with Baltic and eelgrass
                  resolute as maths

      summer's done
    a runner on a budget flight
south leaving us hanging on a long
      distance call that was just
          getting interesting

   there's sweat still
 on the clothes in the basket
and stains from the blackberrying
      the jizz of blood and juice
          unwashable and sweet

        the good days
     we number up in conkers
a jar of dulling eyes plucked
      from the trees by our common
          or garden Ulysses
       the bad days
   we bury in the trash with
final demands and sticky bones
   human remains of the last
      chance barbeque

        bonfire smoke
     slips over next door's
privet hedge like the victim's shift
      from a Hammer vampire flick
        in the grip of Arctic

The Night Watch Man

He calls them the Low Countries
because his hope has been flattened
beyond the rind of gull-stricken dykes
where the sea back home is waiting.

Then he meets her, in front of a rope
in Room 2.8 at the Rijksmuseum
where she's watching Rembrandt
who fixes her with a father's eye
like they have just ended a row
and she's been grounded with Art
for a threadless, echoing afternoon.

He asks her where to buy coffee.
Soon they find themselves enfolded
as November smoulders outside
and branches smack the shutters
to scratched Coltrane and warm gin
from cracked cups and plum cake
before night pours in around them.

Later he discovers the old man's face
wedged in her bathroom mirror
on a postcard curled with steam
that gaze weighing up a Millennium
of terror, decoration and uniforms,
iPhones, Hiroshimas and Hello Kitty
saying "Only Gods can change."

In his black stare, a Pole Star flares
by which her love makes navigation
and gives berth to stowaways sailing
every depth but the sea back home.

Have we won yet?

The soldier grows cold in the sun.
Lawn stripes down to the bright marquee.
Roses fanfare glory from the borders.
In the terrible clatter of cups and saucers
he hears the chipped symphony of England
officially at peace with everything but itself.
He's put on a bit of weight in Civvy Street
the kind that sits on the shoulders
for which there's no diet or training plan.
The roses grow the same in Afghanistan
scented, he remembers, like his Gran.
He pressed one in a copy of Men's Fitness
watched it darken, before sending it
in a card, but she'd died before Christmas.
(There was always something back home
they weren't telling him about Love.)
In Kandahar, it's what blooms underfoot
that will fuck you up, no going back
no more Big Billy Sunshine to the mates.
He pulls the Black Watch tartan rug
over his steel and plastic legs and wonders
what counts as Heroic in summertime.

A Page of Revelation

In a miracle of flash bulbs, the Pontiff rolls up on casters,
spiritual muscle either side, packing heat and earpieces.
A young nuncio-in-shades whispers the old German inside
towards the pink swell of Heaven's voices filling the helix
of Gaudi's Sagrada Familia: he will be the first Pope to enter
but he stops - transfixed by the granite tortoise grinning
under its column, catching his eye, another beady primitive
with the Church on his back moving with the certainty of silt.
His gaze lifts to the Door of the Nativity opening eastwards,
stone-hooded with an Annunciation and buttressed
by bio-gothic labials studded with sculptural fecundity:
grapes and palms and lobster claws, anemones and seahorses,
tumbling melons, wheat sheaves, mangoes, salamanders,
starfish, a sardine's spine, a tributary of pomegranates,
all sluicing towards the Virgin's gape, where the sun rises
at the corner of the sea in the middle of the world.
Maybe he recalls the day as a brown-shirted cub in Bavaria
unfurling the wiry engraving of The Vulva labelled FIG. 1
smudged in a much thumbed Encyclopaedia Germanica
which he now sees for the first time in three dimensions
and touches light as a lover who returns from a distant war,
flesh to rock, rock to flesh, ashes to ashes, dust to dust.
A double consecration.

This is not a scam

Dear Occupier,
You may be an heir to a major fortune
as I have recently been contacted
by a well-wisher with your interests at heart
who would prefer to remain anonymous.

We do not require any money right now
nor do we need your bank account details.
This is a genuine opportunity for you
to become rich beyond your wildest dreams.

At this stage, I cannot go into details.
To explain what this legacy may be worth
just walk outside your front door today
and pick up the nearest blade of grass.

Crush it in your palm and feel the microvolt
of chlorophyll prickle your skin.
Scrunch it nasally and shazam your brain
with blazing lawns and zebra shade.

Find one of those park benches with slats.
Lie face down and gaze at the world below
at the beetling of weeds, cartons and glass
sharded into sun charms, freely scattered.

Settle yourself in the fiercest nettle bed.
Pinch off one of the tiny white flutes
and suck the pith of a zillion molecules
whistling through its sweet gills.

Finally, you may wish to rip off your shirt
to hurtle through leaves like you were tusked
or horned or beaked, bellowing so hard
the studs of your beating lungs pop out.

Naturally, you will be ridiculed for sniffing
sun-baked bricks or stroking wads of moss.
You will be wrenched from attending larks
to be parked instead in front of Twitter or TV.

Which is why you need KARMA-GUARD.
Formulated by renowned Kismeticians
at the University of Om, one spray a day
protects you from casual Weltschmertz.

Just visit www.allaboutyouraura.com

Serenely yours, Gilgamesh P. Stratocaster

P.S. This is not a scam.

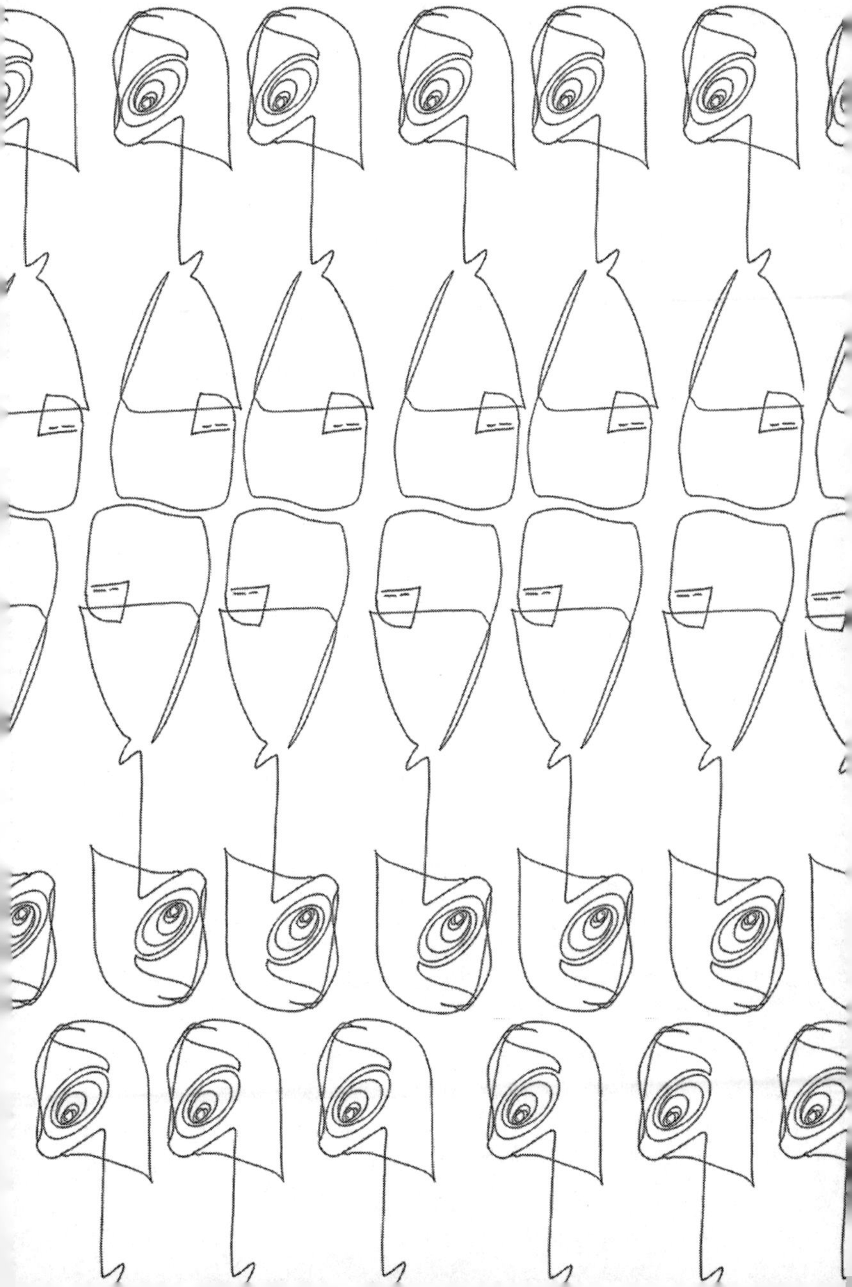

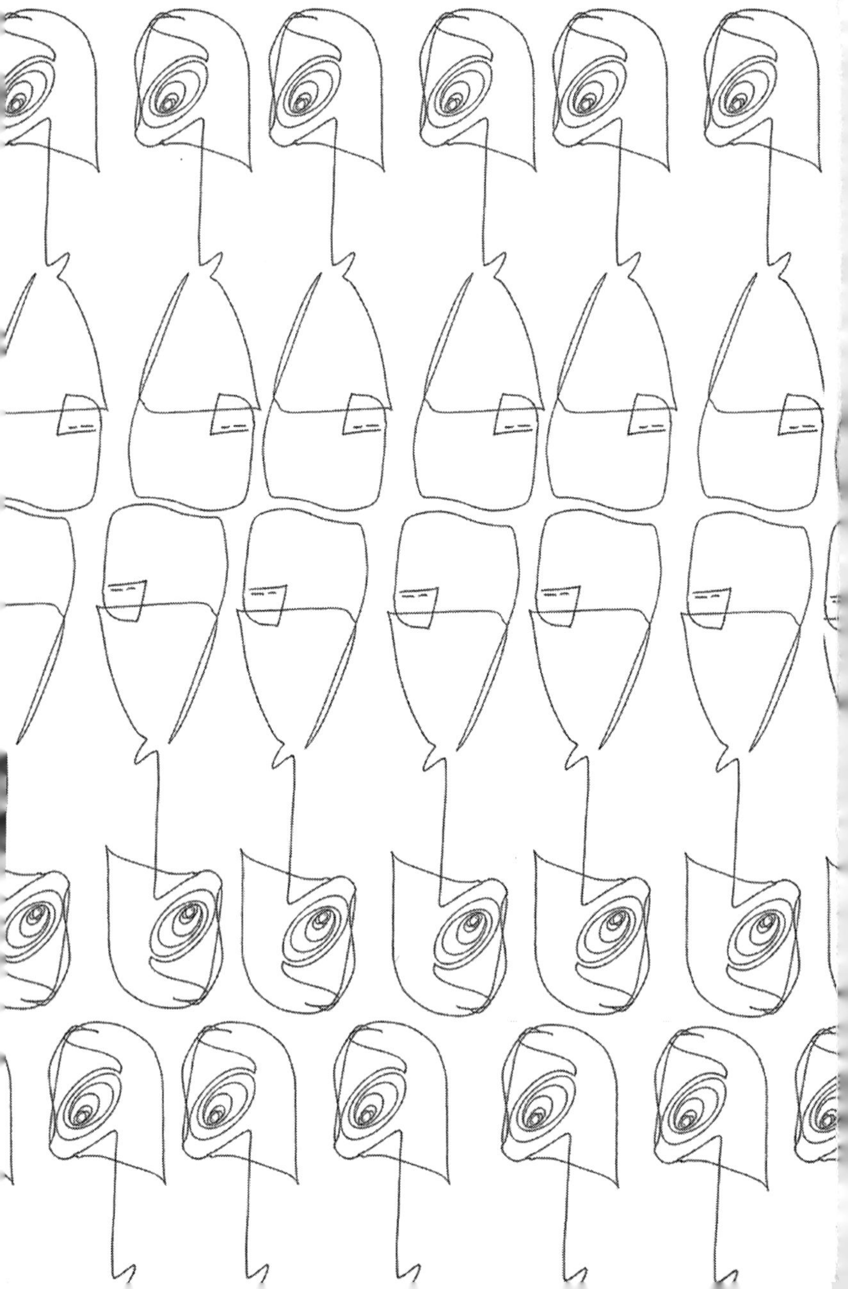